Eat for Hormone Balance

16 Female Hormone Balance Foods

By

Nicole Heath

Introduction

UNDERSTANDING YOUR HORMONES AND HOW THEY GET OUT OF BALANCE

It's easy to overlook in this time and age that the nutrients we eat build every single cell in our bodies. All of our hormones and neurotransmitters, which influence how we feel every day, are made from the proteins, lipids, vitamins, and minerals we consume.

Hormones in women are a complicated system that must be maintained in a precise balance. Women's hormones, on the other hand, are heavily influenced by nutrition, exercise, sleep, stress levels, and environmental pollutants. As a result, a minor hormonal imbalance can become the root cause of a variety of health issues, including irregular periods, acne, PCOS, thyroid disorders, and chronic fatigue.

Hormonal imbalances occur when the bloodstream contains less or more of a hormone. Because hormones perform such an important role in the body, even mild hormonal abnormalities could have far implications.

Hormones are chemicals produced by the endocrine system's glands. Hormones enter the bloodstream to the tissues and organs, carrying messages that direct the organs on what to do and when to do it.

Because hormones are involved in the regulation of the majority of major bodily processes, a hormonal imbalance can have an impact on a wide range of bodily functions.

Hormones aid in the regulation of

- Metabolism and appetite.
- The heart rate
- Sleeping patterns
- Sexual function and reproductive cycles
- Growth and development in general
- Mood and level of stress
- The body's temperature

Insulin, steroid, growth hormone, and adrenaline imbalances can affect both men and women.

Women may also experience estrogen and progesterone imbalances, whereas men are more likely to experience testosterone imbalances.

Sex Hormones

Our sex hormones regulate reproduction, the development of sex traits (for example, breasts and hips), and sexual motivation. Estrogen, progesterone, and testosterone are three of the most important hormones.

How Do They Get Out of Balance?

Our sex hormone levels might alter naturally as we age (for example, during puberty or menopause), but they can also become imbalanced by nutrition, lifestyle, and contaminants.

Hormones of the thyroid

Thyroid hormones are in charge of energy and metabolism. T3, T4, and calcitonin are among them. TSH, which is produced in the pituitary gland, aids in thyroid regulation.

How Do They Get Out of Balance?

Iodine insufficiency, failure to create adequate amounts of thyroid hormones, autoimmunity in which the body attacks thyroid tissue, and thyroid growth

Adrenaline hormones

The adrenal glands are situated above the kidneys. They aid in stress management, blood sugar and blood pressure regulation, and the production of sex hormones. Cortisol, adrenaline, DHEA, aldosterone, and norepinephrine are examples of adrenal hormones.

How Do They Get Out of Balance?

Severe physical and emotional stress, little sleep, and bad nutrition (including excessive sugar, which sets off blood sugar imbalance).

Symptoms of Hormonal Imbalance

Bloating, fatigue, irritability, hair loss, palpitations, mood swings, blood sugar issues, difficulty concentrating, and infertility are just a few symptoms of hormone imbalance. These compounds have an impact on every cell and system in the body. Hormone imbalance can be crippling. Some hormonal changes, such as monthly fluctuations in sex hormones responsible for the menstrual cycle and ovulation, or changes that occur during pregnancy, are normal. Menopause is also another time in a woman's life when she experiences a normal hormonal shift. During this time, many women often experience weight gain, changes in mood, night sweats, and decreased sex drive. These fluctuations can also be caused by a medication or a medical condition.

Kale

Many dangerous toxins, such as pesticides, heavy metals, and pollutants, are absorbed by the body from the environment. These are known as endocrine disrupters, and they are extremely dangerous to our health because they disrupt the balance of our hormones.

Organic kale aids in the detoxification of these chemicals from our liver, thereby aiding in the balance of our hormones. Kale is high in fiber, which feeds the good bacteria in your gut. According to research, friendly gut flora may play an important role in removing estrogen from your system and promoting hormone balance. Fiber can also help with insulin sensitivity and feelings of fullness.

Kale is high in magnesium, which helps maintain healthy levels of estrogen and testosterone. Low hormone levels have been associated with a higher risk of insulin resistance, type 2 diabetes, and heart disease in both men and women.

Cinnamon

Energy, fertility, sleep, appetite (and more) are all regulated by a good hormonal system, which is why hormonal imbalances and swings can cause a wide range of symptoms.

Period cramps and heavy flow have been reported to be greatly reduced in women who take Cinnamon For individuals who experience heavy bleeding during menstruation. Ceylon cinnamon bark is a delicious spice that helps to prevent excessive bleeding by increasing blood circulation.

When hormones are out of balance, such as with polycystic ovary syndrome, periods and ovulation could become irregular or disappear.

A 2014 study found that women with PCOS who ate cinnamon had more frequent menstrual cycles and regular ovulation than women who took a placebo (American Journal of Obstetrics and Gynecology).

When blood sugar levels fall too low, the stress hormone cortisol is secreted (for instance after a big insulin surge). With 1 serving, you can keep your levels stable.

Furthermore, mood swings can occur when large insulin surges remove so much sugar from the blood that energy levels plummet dramatically. Cinnamon has been shown to help lower blood sugar levels after eating (Diabetes, Obesity, and Metabolism, 2009), thereby reducing insulin overproduction and the resulting moodiness.

Avocado

Excessive junk food consumption can result in an elevated insulin level in the body.

This can harm the pituitary gland in the brain and disrupt the endocrine system as a whole.

Avocado is one of the healthiest superfoods for insulin regulation and ovulation regulation.

Avocado contains a lot of fiber and healthy fats. Avocado has been shown in studies to reduce estrogen absorption while increasing testosterone levels.

Avocados may also benefit your heart health, according to research. Consume avocados in moderation because they are high in calories. A good serving size to aim for is one-fourth of an avocado per day.

Walnuts

Walnuts, which contain iodine and selenium, are very healthy nuts that help to balance female hormones.

Selenium is an essential nutrient that has been linked to the prevention of goiters and thyroid gland swelling. A small handful of nuts per day is extremely beneficial to the body.

Apple Cider Vinegar

Apple cider vinegar aids digestion and allows you to absorb more nutrients for better overall health.

Pour one tablespoon of apple cider vinegar into a glass of water.

Broccoli

Broccoli has a big influence on our hormone balance. This is because of how it affects how the body breaks down estrogen. Sulforaphane is another essential component of broccoli. Sulforaphane is being extensively researched for its potential use in the treatment of cancer and other diseases. It also aids in the treatment of fatty liver disease and increases detoxification pathways in the liver, which are essential for estrogen metabolism. Broccoli is also high in potassium, calcium, and magnesium. These are some essential minerals that promote muscle function and bone strength.

Green Tea

Green tea has numerous health benefits, which most people are aware of. In addition, it increases metabolism in the body. Green tea contains theanine, a compound that lowers cortisol levels, a stress hormone. It also contains antioxidants, which help to reduce inflammation and the risk of disease.

Flax Seeds

Flax seeds are nutrient- and fiber-rich seeds that also have hormone-balancing properties due to the presence of special compounds known as "lignans." Lignans can be found in a variety of fiber-rich foods, including other;

- Oilseeds,
- Whole grains,
- Legumes, and
- Some vegetables.

But flax seeds are the most well-known source of these compounds.

If you have symptoms of estrogen dominance, and especially if you suffer from constipation, you should prioritize this superfood (meaning, less than one bowel movement a day).

Flax seeds help to balance hormones in two ways. To begin with, lignins bind to estrogen in the intestine, making sure that those estrogens are excreted in the feces. This "interrupts" estrogen reabsorption back into the bloodstream through the liver, allowing us to lower the body's overall estrogen levels. This is great for women suffering from estrogen dominance.

Furthermore, lignans increase the liver's production of Sex Hormone Binding Globulin (SHBG). The more SHBG we have circulating in our blood, the more it binds to estrogen, making it less available for binding to receptors and contributing to estrogen dominant symptoms.

In one study, 18 women's menstrual periods were studied for three cycles on their typical, low-fiber diet, and then for three cycles while supplementing with flaxseed. The flax seed cycles had no anovulatory cycles (compared to a total of three anovulatory cycles in the control), longer luteal phase lengths, and better luteal phase estrogen: progesterone ratios.

My typical hormone-balancing prescription is 2 tablespoons of ground flax seeds per day, though some research suggests that whole flax seeds can also work. I recommend storing your flax seeds in the fridge to preserve the healthy oils and grinding them right before eating. If you don't want to go through the trouble of grinding your flax seeds, you can simply buy pre-ground flax seeds.

Here are some easy ways to incorporate flax into your daily routine:

- Add 1-2 Tbsp. ground flax to your smoothie

- Sprinkle flax seeds on top of your grains or

salads.

Sea Kelp

Sea kelp is one of nature's most effective foods for balancing female hormones. Sea kelp contains a high concentration of iodine. A trace mineral that promotes thyroid gland healing. Kelp is also an excellent source of vitamins and nutrients, including:

- Vitamin K

- Vitamin A
- Calcium
- iron \s
- Magnesium

Kelp has also been shown in studies to have strong anti-cancer properties, particularly against breast and colon cancer. Its high antioxidant levels not only fight free radicals but can also help diabetes patients and act as a powerful anti-inflammatory agent. Because it contains ten times more calcium than milk, sea kelp is ideal for pregnant women.

Fiber

Dietary fiber is known to enhance healthy cholesterol levels, support cardiovascular health, and reduce the risk of colon cancer; it also plays a vital role in hormone health. Insoluble dietary fibers, such as lignin (discussed above and found in flax seeds, but also in the bran layer of grains, beans, and seeds), help bind to estrogen in the intestine and transport it out of the body through the feces. This aids in the reduction or prevention of "estrogen dominant" symptoms.

If you have symptoms of estrogen dominance, especially if you have constipation (less than one bowel movement per day), or if you've been told you have high cholesterol, you should prioritize this superfood.

One study compared the estrogen excretion of vegetarian versus omnivorous women. The vegetarian diet was linked to higher estrogen excretion (measured in the stool), most likely due to the increased fiber content of their nutrition.

Furthermore, fiber is essential in "feeding" our healthy gut bacteria. The more we can feed and promote good bacteria, the less estrogen "reabsorption" occurs in the bloodstream.

As previously stated, dietary fiber increases SHBG, which then binds to estrogen in the bloodstream and aids in the reduction of estrogen-dominant symptoms.

Whole grains, beans, legumes, flax seeds, other seeds, fruits, and vegetables are all high in fiber.

So, how much fiber should you consume daily? Teenagers and women should consume at least 25g of fiber per day. In general, I recommend around 35g per day.

Here are some ideas for increasing your fiber intake:

• Add 2 tablespoons of ground flax seeds to your smoothie or sprinkle on top of grains.

• Choose whole grains over refined white baked goods.

• Toss some nuts and seeds into your salads.

• Aim for at least 8 cups of vegetables per day.

• In the morning, mix 1 tablespoon psyllium husk into your oatmeal.

• Increase the number of beans and legumes in your diet.

• Include higher-fiber fruits such as apples, pears, and apricots.

• Consume a green smoothie every day.

Sea Salt

One of our adrenal hormones, aldosterone, is in charge of fluid balance and blood pressure. When our adrenals aren't working properly and our aldosterone levels drop, we can secrete more sodium, leading to salt cravings. A pinch of sea salt sprinkled on your food or in a glass of water will help to replenish sodium levels and provide trace minerals. For their salt content, you can also try seaweed or miso.

Millet
Millet is a gluten-free whole grain that contains a variety of B vitamins that can help our nerves and brains when we are stressed. It also has magnesium and fiber, which help to keep blood sugar levels stable.

Eggs

Grab an egg for a dose of choline, a vitamin that aids in the production of the neurotransmitter acetylcholine, which is necessary for the nervous system, brain health, memory, and development. They also have omega-3 fatty acids, which are anti-inflammatory fats that help the brain. When our minds and nervous systems are in good health, we are better able to deal with stress. Instead of conventional eggs, opt for organic, pasture-raised eggs.

Healthy Carbs
Too many people are put off by the word
"carbohydrates," but not all carbs are created
equal.
Carbohydrates like...
Oats
Quinoa
Buckwheat
Legumes and wild rice
They are not only high in nutrients, but they
also aid in blood sugar regulation.
Why are Healthy Carbohydrates Beneficial for
Hormonal Imbalance?
When the body does not have enough glucose,
it produces cortisol (the stress hormone), which
causes hormonal imbalance and harms the body
at the cellular level.

Whole and unprocessed complex carbohydrates (such as the ones mentioned above) take longer to break down, resulting in a steady stream of glucose that promotes healthy blood sugar levels.

Pumpkin Seeds
Pumpkin seeds are high in magnesium. When we are stressed, our magnesium levels can drop. Magnesium is an anti-stress mineral that works with Vitamin C and B5 to support the adrenal glands and reduce stress levels. In summary, foods high in magnesium, such as pumpkin seeds, can help us relax.

Bell Peppers
These sweet peppers provide us with a boost of Vitamin C, an antioxidant vitamin that is necessary for the adrenal glands to function properly. We have a lot of Vitamin C stored in

our adrenal glands, and when we are stressed, we use a lot of it. Vitamin C-rich foods, such as bell peppers, provide replenishment, as well as a slew of B vitamins that provide energy and aid in stress reduction.

Organic Tempeh
Soy is a contentious topic for a variety of reasons, including genetic modification and allergies, but by selecting high-quality sources such as organic miso and tempeh, you can reap the benefits of soy's flavones, which have phytoestrogenic properties and can lower the risk of breast cancer. A fermented soy product, such as tempeh or miso, will provide you with beneficial probiotics that will improve digestion and mood. Balanced digestive flora also

reduces the activity of an enzyme called beta-glucuronidase, which has been linked to estrogen-related cancers.

Brazil Nuts
Brazil nuts are high in selenium, an antioxidant that helps protect the thyroid gland and aids in the conversion of T4 to T3, the active form of thyroid hormone. Just a couple of Brazil nuts per day will suffice to meet your selenium requirements, and they taste delicious, so it's a no-brainer!

Hormone Boosting Fruits

Fruits can cause an increase in insulin levels, which can impact cortisol and estrogen levels, so they should be consumed in moderation.

When fruits are consumed in sufficient quantities, they can have a positive effect on hormone levels.

Apples

We've all heard the adage "an apple a day keeps the doctor away," but is it true?

Apples can be eaten on the go, chopped up and baked with cinnamon for a sweet but healthy snack, or added to salads and other recipes.

They're not only versatile, but they're also good for your hormones.

Why Are Apples Good for Hormone Imbalance?

Apples are high in vitamin C, which is required for the production of progesterone, the hormone that relieves depression and anxiety.

Furthermore, apples contain a powerful antioxidant known as quercetin, which can help to increase the antioxidant capacity of the ovaries.

Blueberries

Blueberries are tasty and nutritious, and they can be consumed daily as part of a healthy and balanced diet.

For good reason, this tiny berry is quickly becoming one of the most popular superfoods.

Why Are Blueberries Good for Hormone Imbalance?

They may be small, but these little berries have come to fight... for your health.

Blueberries are high in vitamin C and potassium, as well as flavonoids and antioxidants, making them an excellent fighter against inflammation, cancer, and heart disease.

But what can they do to assist you with your hormonal imbalance?

They're also high in vitamin B6, which helps with progesterone production and balance.

Strawberries
Strawberries are a refreshing summer treat that can be eaten all year. They can be included in your:

Cereal

Oatmeal

Smoothie

and even a protein bowl

Salads

They are not only delicious, but they are also effective in the fight against hormonal imbalances.

Why Are Strawberries Good for Hormone Imbalance?

Strawberries not only have high levels of phytoestrogens, which can help with hormonal balance, but they're also high in vitamin C, which helps improve health and stabilize hormones.

Hormone balance Salad with Kale

2 portions

50g Brussels sprouts

1 pound of cranberries

3 tbsp. Mustard Dijon

1/3 cup cider vinegar

9 tbsp. walnut oil

Kale 30g (pre-cooked)

1 tbsp. crumbled feta cheese

Chestnuts, 100g

A handful of parsley

A quarter avocado, sliced

A few chopped mint leaves

Seeds of pomegranate

2 tbsp. agave

To serve as a garnish, sprinkle with cress.

Instructions

1 Trim, chop and blanch the sprouts for 2 minutes before cooling them in ice water and drying them off.

2 Cook cranberries in a saucepan with water until tender, then blend and strain through a sieve.

3 Combine the mustard, vinegar, and cranberry in a mixing bowl, then slowly drizzle in the oil and season with salt and pepper to taste.

4 Toss the sprouts with the remaining ingredients, then drizzle with the dressing and season to taste.

5 Garnish with a few cress sprigs and serve.

Salad with Kale and Quinoa to Support Hormones

2 portions

Ingredients

2 bunches chopped lacinato kale

Quinoa (cooked) 2/3 cup

½ large, thinly sliced apple

1/4 cup unsalted walnuts

1/4 cup pumpkin seeds, uncooked

3 tbsp. dried cranberries, 1 tbsp. hemp hearts

Avocado oil for dressing

Lemon juice, freshly squeezed

Sea salt

Instructions

In a large serving bowl, combine chopped kale and tbsp fresh lemon juice. Massage the kale leaves with lemon juice for about 2 minutes, or until they begin to soften. Allow 10 minutes for the lemon juice to break down some of the fibers in the leaves.

Toss the remaining salad ingredients into a serving bowl. Drizzle the salad with the desired amount of avocado oil and lemon juice, then season with sea salt. Toss everything together until it's well combined. Enjoy!

Overnight Oats for Hormone Balance

Ingredients

Gluten-free pinhead oats 160g/534 oz 440ml (134 cups) nut milk

Hemp seeds (30g/1 oz)

30g/1 oz pecans (or other nuts of your choice)

30g desiccated coconut (1 oz)

A smear of unsweetened coconut yogurt

1 tbsp chia seeds

Optional: 1 scoop vanilla protein powder, 2 teaspoons sugar-free maple syrup

Served with: Blueberries, raspberries, and coconut flakes

Instructions:

In a large mixing bowl, combine all of the ingredients and stir well to ensure that the protein powder is well incorporated and not lumpy.

Place in glass jars or toxin-free Tupperware and refrigerate overnight to soften the pinhead oats. They'll be chewing on the first day, but they'll soften up with each passing day!

To serve, top with berries and coconut flakes.

If your yogurt has a short shelf life, skip this step and stir in just before serving to keep the overnight oats from spoiling.

Shot of Broccoli Sprouts

Broccoli sprouts are a superfood that helps to balance hormones. This tonic is an excellent way to reverse estrogen dominance using a simple healing food.

Sprouts of cruciferous seeds are extremely estrogen-balancing. 1-2 tbsp per day is a good starting point. Lemon juice is extremely alkalizing to the body. Also, salt is excellent for rehydrating.

½ cup servings

Ingredients

½ cup broccoli sprigs

½ cup of filtered water

1 lemon, 1 pinch sea salt (about 2 tablespoons)

Instructions

In a high-speed blender, combine all of the sprouts and blend until bright green. Serve right away.

Fresh is best, but leftovers should be refrigerated for no more than a day.

Smoothie Bowl with Berries

If you're looking for something packed with antioxidants and healthy fats for breakfast, then this smoothie bowl is for you!

Smoothies provide all of the healthy fats, fiber, and antioxidants required for happy, healthy hormones.

Ingredients:

1 cup fresh blueberries

A banana cut in half

2 tablespoons ground flax seeds

Cinnamon pinch

A pinch of sea salt

1 Vega Sport Vanilla or Bulletproof Collagen Vanilla scoop

1 tablespoon of your preferred nut butter

1 coconut milk cup

Goji berries, a handful

A handful of walnuts

A quarter cup rolled oats

Instructions

Blend until smooth, then top with goji berries, oats, and walnuts, or whatever toppings you prefer!

Strawberry smoothie for hormone balance

1.5 servings

Ingredients

1 1/2 cup frozen strawberries (or berries of your choice!)

1 ripe banana

1 cup purified water

1 teaspoon chia seeds

1 tsp cacao powder, unsweetened

1/2 teaspoon maca powder

A few handfuls of spinach

Three Brazil nuts

Optional: 1 scoop collagen (omit if vegetarian or vegan)

Toppings

Pistachios and coconut flakes

Instructions

Blend all of the ingredients!

Enjoy your toppings!

Brazil Nuts Recipes Made Simple

Ingredients

8 servings

A third cup of Brazil nuts (chopped in a food processor)

A third of a cup of pecans (chopped in a food processor)

1/3 cup pumpkin seeds (pepitas)

2 tablespoons ground chia seeds

A third of a cup of flaxseed meal (ground)

1 tablespoon unsweetened coconut flakes

1/3 cup seedless raisins (sultana)

5 tablespoons coconut oil (melted)

4 tablespoons maple syrup

1 teaspoon pure vanilla extract

2 teaspoon cinnamon

Instructions

Preheat the oven to 180 degrees Fahrenheit (82 degrees Celsius).

In a mixing bowl, combine all of the nuts, seeds, and coconut flakes.

In a small mixing bowl, combine melted coconut oil, maple syrup, vanilla extract, and cinnamon.

Pour into the dry ingredients and stir until evenly coated.

Cook for 30 minutes in a preheated oven.

Best Herbs for Hormone Balancing

Herbs are a type of plant whose leaves, flowers, roots, and seeds have a variety of uses.

If you enjoy cooking, you're probably most familiar with the use of herbs as a cooking ingredient. Interestingly, humans have used them for thousands of years for healthcare, spiritual rituals, and other purposes.

Some herbs have even been used in the past to balance hormone levels. Despite the lack of intensive research on the subject, some evidence suggests that certain herbs may influence hormone levels in the body, as well as other endocrine system functions.

Even so, it can be difficult to separate fact from fiction when it comes to using herbs for medical or health purposes.

That's why I looked through the studies and came up with this list of five herbs, each of which has evidence to back up some of its hormone-balancing claims.

Nigella sativa seeds

Nigella sativa is also known as kalonji and fennel flower. Its flowers produce tiny black antioxidant-rich seeds. Because they contain thymoquinone, a phytonutrient or plant compound, these seeds are medicinal.

In people with polycystic ovarian syndrome, researchers are investigating the protective and therapeutic effects of nigella seed (PCOS). PCOS is a condition that causes abnormal hormone levels in women of reproductive age, among other symptoms.

Nigella seed extracts have been proven in animal experiments to help regulate insulin, testosterone, luteinizing hormone, and thyroid hormone levels, among other things.

Additionally, Nigella sativa extract contains estrogenic activity, which means it works in the same way as the hormone estrogen in your body. In fact, some rat studies are looking into whether nigella seed extracts could be used as a substitute to hormone replacement therapy (HRT) during menopause when the body produces less estrogen than it used to.

Concentrated Nigella sativa supplements are gaining popularity and are sometimes marketed as "black seed" or "black cumin seed." Whole nigella seeds have a herbaceous aroma and are simple to incorporate into bread, salads, and other dishes.

However, note that most research on nigella seeds and hormones was conducted in animals and used concentrated extracts or isolated thymoquinone.

As a result, while cooking with whole seeds can be healthy and delicious, it may not provide the same benefits.

Ashwagandha
Ashwagandha is an evergreen shrub in the nightshade family that is also known as winter cherry, Indian ginseng, or Withania somnifera. Many ashwagandha supplements, teas, and root powders are widely available in herbal medicine.

This adaptogen is thought to help your body overcome stress by modulating the hypothalamic-pituitary-adrenal (HPA) axis in the brain. The HPA axis excretes a variety of hormones, which include cortisol, that kickstart your body's response to stress.
Cortisol is a stress hormone that helps you get through stressful and event-filled days.
However, human and rat studies suggest that a chronic imbalance of the hormone may cause endocrine disorders such as Addison's disease and Cushing's syndrome.

A 2019 study of 60 adults found that taking 125–300 mg of ashwagandha root extract twice daily for 8 weeks resulted in less stress, better sleep, and lower blood cortisol levels when compared to a placebo group. A 2012 study with a similar design found comparable results.

Other hormones may be affected by ashwagandha as well. For example, scientists are investigating how it affects insulin levels, reproductive hormones, and other factors.

An 8-week 2018 study in adults with elevated levels of thyroid-stimulating hormone (TSH), which is produced by your pituitary gland and used to assess thyroid problems, discovered that ingesting 600 mg of pure ashwagandha extract daily lowered TSH levels.

However, when it comes to the health advantages of ashwagandha, some research has produced inconsistent results.

During clinical trials, people have also experienced negative effects with ashwagandha supplements, and ashwagandha may be harmful to pregnant and breastfeeding women, as well as those with autoimmune diseases or thyroid issues.

Black cohosh root

Black cohosh is a member of the same plant family as Nigella sativa, which is also known as the crowfoot or buttercup family. Bugbane and rattleweed are other names for black cohosh.

It is a well-known supplement derived from the ground roots of the black cohosh plant. It's usually taken in the form of a capsule, an extract, or a tea.

The herb's medicinal value is thought to be derived from triterpene glycosides, though it's unclear how many of these are present in black cohosh supplements.

Black cohosh has been and continues to be used to help women's health issues such as menstrual irregularities, premenstrual syndrome (PMS), and menopausal symptoms.

Black cohosh, like Nigella sativa, may act as a phytoestrogen — a plant substance that, when consumed in large quantities, acts similarly to the hormone estrogen. However, it is unclear whether black cohosh is a true phytoestrogen or works through other mechanisms.

Several studies have found that black cohosh relieves menopausal symptoms more effectively than a placebo or no treatment at all.

Nonetheless, more rigorous human studies are required, especially given reports of negative –

and even severe – side effects from black cohosh. As a result, it's best to consult with a doctor before using the herb.

Chasteberry

Chasteberry is another popular herbal supplement that can be found in extract or capsule form.

It is frequently combined with other herbs, such as black cohosh, and marketed as a remedy for menopausal symptoms and reproductive health in women.

Chaste berries are the fruit of the Vitex Agnus tree, also known as chaste tree, monk's pepper, or vitex.

The berries' diterpenoid compounds may be responsible for the supplement's potential effects on hormones like prolactin and the neurotransmitter dopamine. Several studies have found that chaste berry may lower prolactin levels in the blood. PMS is frequently associated with high levels of this hormone. The supplement may also help with PMS symptoms such as breast pain.

Other studies have looked at the herb's ability to treat infertility and PCOS as well as relieve menopausal symptoms.

Though it appears that chaste berry may help balance certain hormones such as prolactin, many scientists agree that more human research is needed before drawing any conclusions about its efficacy.

Marjoram
Marjoram and other Origanum genus herbal shrubs, such as oregano, have long been used in traditional medicine to treat a variety of ailments.

The herb contains bioactive plant compounds such as flavonoids and phenolic acids, which are likely responsible for some of its medicinal properties.

Marjoram has been studied in humans and animals to see if it can reduce stress and help people with PCOS.

A recent study, for example, discovered that rats with PCOS who were treated with marjoram extract had higher levels of estradiol — a hormone produced by the ovaries.

In addition, in one small human study, people with PCOS were given marjoram tea twice daily for one month. Marjoram tea was associated with significant reductions in fasting insulin hormone levels when compared to the placebo treatment, which could indicate improved blood sugar management.

However, it is too soon to say how marjoram should be used as an herbal supplement to treat hormonal imbalances. Furthermore, some scientists warn that there is relatively little research on the long-term or intensive use of hormone-altering herbs.

Conclusion

The human body's hormone levels are constantly changing. There are numerous reasons why they fluctuate daily, and those ups and downs are necessary to some extent. Long-term hormonal imbalances, on the other hand, may have an impact on your health.

Eating healthy hormone balance foods is one of many ways to address such changes in blood hormone levels. Each of the foods, fruits, beverages, and herbs discussed in this book has the potential to help balance your hormone levels.

Made in United States
Troutdale, OR
11/25/2024

25257191R00031